Tell me about...

Field Athletics

Published in 2010 by Evans Publishing Ltd,
2A Portman Mansions,
Chiltern St, London WIU 6NR

Editor: Nicola Edwards
Designer: D.R. Ink
All photography by Wishlist except for p6 Matthew Stockman/Getty Images; p9 Michael Steele/Getty Images;
p12 JOHN MACDOUGALL/AFP/Getty Images; p13 Getty Images/Getty Images for Aviva; p24 Shutterstock;
p25 Shutterstock; p26 ADRIAN DENNIS/AFP/Getty Images; p27 Michael Steele/Getty Images

British Library Cataloguing in Publication Data

Gifford, Clive.
  Field athletics. -- (Tell me about sport)
  1. Track and field--Juvenile literature.
  I. Title II. Series
  796.4'2-dc22

ISBN-13: 9780237541545

Printed in China.

The author and publisher would like to thank Sam Prickett, Stephanie Owen, Gregor Kelling
and Sharon Achia, coach Ros Kelling and Banbury Harriers Athletic Club for their help with
the photographs for this book.

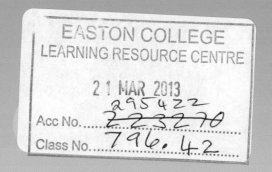

Contents

Field athletics

US athlete Brian Clay arches his back to clear the high jump bar during a decathlon competition. Clay won an Olympic gold medal in the decathlon in 2008.

There is much more to athletics than running races on the track. The sport of field athletics is made up of exciting throwing, jumping and vaulting events. They are among the oldest sporting activities in the world. Many were part of the Ancient Greek Olympics that began over 2,700 years ago.

Field athletics events push competitors to the limit. They need strength but also speed, timing and great skill. Top field athletes train incredibly hard to succeed in the sport. Often only a few centimetres of height or distance separate the best-placed competitors in an event.

Field athletics events are part of multi-sport competitions as well. For example, the women's heptathlon has three

▲ Long jump competitions are often a feature of school sports days.

running races and four field events (long jump, high jump, javelin throw and shot put). The men's ten-event decathlon includes those four field events as well as the pole vault and discus.

You can take part in many field athletics events at school or in after school clubs and athletics competitions. Local athletics clubs often have junior sections and run open days for budding athletes. You can also test yourself by setting up your own simple competitions for throws and jumps with friends.

▲ These competitors are taking part in a cricket ball throwing contest.

Aims and rules

Field athletics events are quite simple to follow. The aim is to vault or jump higher or longer or throw further than other competitors. Athletes must follow the rules of their events to achieve a 'legal' jump or throw. These rules include not stepping over the take-off line in the long jump or the scratch line in the javelin. If they do step over these lines, an official will signal a no jump or no throw.

In all events, athletes are allowed a number of attempts to throw or jump their best distance. Things are

▼ This young athlete is thrilled at breaking her personal best in the high jump. All her training and hard work has been worth it.

▼ This official signals a no throw because the thrower has stepped over the scratch line. Her throw will not count in the competition.

8

Records and bests

In 2001, Gerd Kanter's personal best in the discus was 60.47 metres. He improved it by over 13m in the next few years to become 2008 Olympic champion.

Athletes set world records for the greatest heights or distances ever achieved. No one has got near Jan Zelezny's 1996 javelin record of 98.48m. Zelezny has thrown over 90 metres an amazing 34 times.

▲ Officials measure the distance travelled by a legal throw in the shot put event. At major competitions, the distance is displayed on an electronic scoreboard.

▲ Yelena Isinbayeva rises to set a new pole vault world record in 2008 of 5.03 metres. Isinbayeva has broken the world record many times and in 2009, set a new record of 5.06 metres.

different in the high jump and pole vault. In these events the bar is set at a certain height. Any athlete who clears that height without knocking off the bar is given the chance to jump with the bar set higher. The competition continues until only one jumper clears a height.

As athletes develop, they set themselves target heights or distances to achieve. A personal best (PB) is the best ever height or distance a field athlete has achieved. An SB (season's best) means that they have recorded their best performance of the year.

Field and kit

Field events take place on an athletics field or in an athletics stadium. Each event has its own dedicated area. Athletes make their throws from certain places in these areas: circles for the discus, hammer and shot put and a long strip called a runway for the javelin. To be legal a throw must land inside a fan-shaped area called the landing sector, otherwise the officials will signal a no throw.

▼ These field athletes are warming up their bodies and muscles by jogging. They will perform stretches of their key muscle groups before attempting throws or jumps.

▲ This official is raking the sand of the long jump pit to leave it smooth for the next jumper.

▼ Older and more experienced field athletes wear specialised clothing. Discus shoes (left) have rubber soles for grip whilst javelin shoes have extra support for the ankles.

▲ Always carry the shot with two hands when you are walking around with it between throws. A shot dropped on a foot will definitely break bones!

For athletes who are just beginning to take part in field athletics events, clothing and kit are simple. They wear a vest or t-shirt tucked into running shorts and good, comfortable trainers. It's useful to wear a tracksuit to keep you warm before and after your event. Elite athletes wear specialised clothing and footwear designed for their events.

Equipment such as the high jump posts and bar and the throwing objects are normally provided by your school or athletics club. Your teacher or coach will point out all the safety rules. Make sure you follow them. These include carrying throwing objects carefully, never wandering across landing sectors and never high jumping without a crash mat.

Star athletes

Elite field athletes are rarely as well-known as stars of track athletics but they are still champion performers and some do become famous.

Professional athletes may be given funding to train and compete by schemes run by their country's athletics organisations. Many of the best earn sponsorship money from companies and win appearance fees and prize money at major competitions such as Grand Prix meetings.

▼ The Czech Republic's Barbora Špotáková launches an enormous javelin throw of 72.28 metres at the 2008 World Athletics Final. Her throw was a new world record.

▲ Triple jumper Phillips Idowu trains hard during a 2008/09 winter athletics camp. Idowu became world champion in 2009.

Top athletes work very closely with their coaches who may instruct and train them throughout their careers. From time to time athletes may have to deal with frustrations such as losses of form, defeats and injuries as they push themselves to perform at their best.

Most of the time, top field athletes attend meetings and competitions as individuals. But for major international events such as the Olympics, the European Championships and the Pan-American and Asian Games, they compete as part of a national team, proudly representing their country.

Star moments

At the 2008 World Athletics Final, any field athlete who broke a world record would receive 100,000 US dollars. Barbara Špotáková scooped the prize with a huge javelin throw of 72.28 metres.

Triple jumper Tatyana Lebedeva won a million dollar jackpot in 2005 for winning the triple jump at all six Golden League athletics meetings.

The shot put

The shot put is often the first throwing event young field athletes learn. It takes place inside a throwing circle which has a wooden board at the front, called a stopboard.

Competitors in the shot put must enter and leave the circle from the back. They start at the back of the circle holding the shot with their body in a low position and finish at the front of the circle in a high position.

The power in the putting attempt comes not just from the arm but from the whole body, with the legs driving up and forward as they move across the circle.

▼ The shot put circle is 2.135 metres wide. The wooden stopboard allows throwers to brace their front foot against it, to stop them toppling out of the circle.

▼ This thrower begins his shot put attempt by cradling the shot into his neck. He holds the shot on his three middle fingers, not clutched in his palm.

▲ This young athlete is learning to put the shot from a standing position. Her putting arm drives through, passing her head. Her elbow stays high as she releases the shot.

Athletes need great strength and skilful technique to propel the shot large distances. Top shot putters can send the heavy shot over 20 metres. They use two different techniques to move from the back of the circle to the front. Some perform a full turn of their bodies in the circle to make their throw. Others use the O'Brien technique, hopping in a straight line across the circle.

▶

This athlete releases the shot with a flick of her fingers forwards and upwards.

The long jump

The long jump starts with a strong, smooth sprint down a long strip of track called the runway. It is followed by a big leap from a take-off board into a sandpit.

The long jump is one of the easiest field athletics events for beginners to attempt, but you need good speed on the runway and great jumping technique to gain plenty of distance.

You need to pace your run-up carefully so that you do not overstep the take-off board. Overstepping the board would mean that your jump would not count.

◀ A long jumper sprints down the runway uncurling from a low body position at the start to running upright and fast.

▲ This long jumper leaps powerfully, extending his arms and legs ahead of his body. As he lands he will collapse his legs, bending at the knees to land as far forward in the sand as possible.

Once long jumpers have left the ground, they can use several different techniques in the air. Some prefer the sail technique in which both feet are lifted up in front of the body. Others prefer to cycle their legs through the air – the hitch kick technique. The aim of all the techniques is to move through the air above the sand for as long as possible before landing.

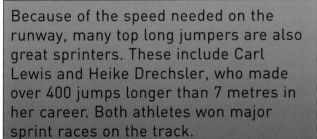

Great long jumpers

Because of the speed needed on the runway, many top long jumpers are also great sprinters. These include Carl Lewis and Heike Drechsler, who made over 400 jumps longer than 7 metres in her career. Both athletes won major sprint races on the track.

The famous sprinter Jesse Owens also held the long jump record of 8.13m for an amazing 25 years.

Mike Powell holds the men's world record of 8.95m. The women's world record is 7.52m by Galina Chistyakova.

▼ A long jump is measured from the take-off board to the nearest point in the sand that the jumper touches. This is why it is very important to not lean back and place your hands behind you on landing.

Take-off board

The high jump

The high jump bar is placed on two supports fitted to poles called uprights which are four metres apart. A large crash mat is usually placed behind the poles so that jumpers can land safely on it. Jumpers may knock the bar and make it wobble but if it falls, their jump has failed.

High jumpers are usually allowed three attempts to jump over the bar at a set height. If they fail all three attempts, they are out. This makes the event exciting and dramatic for spectators but tense for competitors who know that the smallest mistake could ruin their chances of success.

▶

The simplest high jump technique is called the scissors because of the shape the legs make as they clear the bar. This jumper tries to keep her back straight as her legs cross the bar in front of her body.

High jump facts

The only person to have jumped higher than a football goal crossbar is Cuba's Javier Sotomayor. He has cleared a height of 2.30m or more in over 200 different competitions.

Blanka Vlašić won 34 competitions in a row prior to the 2008 Olympics in which she had to settle for a silver medal.

▲ This high jumper looks over his shoulder, arches his back and raises his hips high to clear the bar. He will hitch his feet up to make sure that they don't rattle the bar.

If more than one jumper is left at the end of a competition with equal heights cleared, the one with the fewest failed attempts wins. At the 2008 Olympics Blanka Vlašić and Tia Hellebaut both cleared 2.05m but because Vlašić had taken an extra attempt to clear that height, Hellebaut won the gold.

There have been different jumping techniques in the past but in the 1960s, an American athlete called Dick Fosbury invented the Fosbury Flop. This is the technique almost all athletes use today.

▼ This jumper performs a Fosbury Flop. She launches off her take-off foot and leaps over the bar head and shoulders first. She lifts her hips and then her legs and feet to make sure she gets over the bar without knocking it off. She lands on her back on the crash mat.

The javelin

The javelin is a pointed pole made of metal or fibreglass, although javelins for beginners are sometimes made of plastic. A full javelin is over two metres long. Athletes must throw the javelin as far as possible after they have completed a run-up along a runway.

To throw the javelin athletes face the front as they run up and then turn to the side in the last strides as they withdraw the javelin. They drive their hip forwards as they turn to face the front again, releasing the javelin powerfully.

▼ You hold a javelin in the cord grip area.

▼ To perform a full throw, you build speed up on the runway. This athlete carries the javelin at head height.

▲ This thrower has pulled the javelin back. With his front leg braced and as straight as possible, his hips and then chest start to turn to face the front. His throwing arm pulls the javelin through. The javelin passes by his head as it is released.

The angle at which an athlete releases the javelin influences how well it flies. Direction is important, too. The javelin must land inside the landing sector and its pointed nose must hit the ground first for the throw to be counted.

◄ This javelin has landed correctly, point-first. If a javelin lands flat on the ground, it is counted as a no throw.

Long-distance throws

Top athletes can throw the javelin huge distances. In 1984, Uwe Hohn threw a staggering 104.80 metres.

In the 1980s and 1990s javelins for men and women were redesigned so that they would fly shorter distances. This was to stop top athletes from endangering spectators with their monster throws.

The discus

The discus was part of the Ancient Olympics as far back as 703BCE. The discus is also the only field event for which the women's world record is longer than the men's. This is because the discus used by women weighs 1kg, half the weight of the men's.

A discus throw takes place in a 2.5m throwing circle. Experienced athletes begin at the back of the circle and use fast, accurate footwork to turn round as they cross the circle, their throwing arm lagging behind.

▼ This discus thrower holds the discus with his fingers spread. He grips its ring with his fingertips.

▼ He builds up a rhythm by swinging his arm holding the discus. He uses his other hand to support the discus.

Discus data

Faina Melnik from the Soviet Union broke the women's discus world record 11 times. In 1975, she was the first woman to throw over 70 metres.

Al Oerter won the men's discus competition in four Olympics in a row (1956-68) but he produced his longest ever throw after his Olympic successes, at the age of 43.

◀ The thrower releases the discus with his shoulders facing the front.

As they face the front of the circle, they brace their left leg and side of their body and whip their arm through. The action is like uncoiling a large spring. They release the discus at about shoulder height with a straight arm.

As the discus leaves the hand, the fingers press down on its edges. This helps it spin away smoothly and travel further. Top throwers practise releasing the discus at the ideal angle to send it flying huge distances – often over 65 metres.

▼ This discus thrower has lost his balance and has stepped out of the front of the circle. His attempt will be a no throw.

Advanced events

There are three exciting field events which you need to be older to take part in. These are the pole vault, the triple jump and the hammer throw.

The pole vault is the most spectacular of all field events. Athletes run down a runway carrying a long pole. They plant one end of the pole in a small box. The pole bends greatly and then straightens, powering each vaulter upwards upside-down.

Field athletics feats

The men's hammer weighs 7.26kg, the women's 4kg. In 1986, Yuriy Sedykh threw the hammer 86.74m. No one has got close to his world record ever since.

Legendary pole vaulter, Sergei Bubka broke the world outdoor record 17 times during his career and was the first athlete to vault 6 metres.

Only five triple jumps have been made over 18 metres and Britain's Jonathan Edwards made four of them. His 1995 world record of 18.29m still stands.

Vaulters have to swivel their body to fly over a high bar without knocking it off.

▶

This pole vaulter is sailing over the bar. She needs careful timing to let go of the pole at the right moment and to make sure that her arms and upper body clear the bar.

The hammer is a heavy metal ball on the end of a chain with a handle. Hammer throwers swing the hammer around the throwing circle before turning three or four times across the circle themselves. Great strength and timing is needed to release the hammer at the right time to send it flying away.

▲ This hammer thrower is making her first swings of the hammer. These swings help to build up speed and rhythm.

The triple jump is a complicated event. It is held on the same runway and pit as the long jump. Triple jumpers have to take off and land on the same foot for the first stage, the hop. Then, they take as big a step as they can before making a jump into the pit.

▼ This triple jumper makes the hop (left), landing on the same foot he took off from. He then makes a large leaping step (centre) before launching off his take-off leg to jump (right) into the sand pit.

The world of field athletics

▲ Ralf Bartels, a shot putter from Germany, begins a throw at the 2009 European Indoor Championships which were held in the Italian city of Turin. Bartels won a bronze medal with a throw of 20.39 metres.

Many athletics meetings feature events for both track and field. These range from local meets through to national championships and major international athletics competitions such the IAAF World Championships which is held every two years.

The athletics season is split into summer and winter competitions. Most winter competitions are held in indoor stadiums and feature a smaller range of field events including the long jump, shot put, high jump and pole vault.

At the peak of the sport is the Olympic Games. Held once every four years, athletes strive to qualify for the competition and then to make the final of their event. Since 2000, when the women's triple jump and pole vault

▲ Russian jumping legend Tatyana Lebedeva leaps to victory in the long jump during the 2007 World Athletics Final in Stuttgart, Germany. Lebedeva is unusual in that she competes regularly in both the triple jump and long jump, having won Olympic medals in both events.

were added, men and women compete in the same number of field events.

The Paralympics is held in the weeks after each Olympics for elite athletes with a disability. Field athletics features highly, including shot put and javelin events for wheelchair-bound competitors and the long jump and triple jump for blind and partially-sighted athletes.

Champion performances

Carl Lewis won the long jump competition at four different Olympic Games, an amazing achievement.

Bulgaria's Stefka Kostadinova won the women's high jump at a record five World Indoor Championships.

At the 2004 World Indoor Championships, Russian triple jumper Tatyana Lebedeva broke the world record three times (15.16m, 15.25m and 15.36m) on her way to the gold medal.

Where next?

There are some good websites and books for you to gain further information on athletics. Ask your coach or sports teacher about athletics schemes in your area.

http://www.iaaf.org/
The International Association of Athletics Federations website is enormous with hundreds of biographies of leading athletes and details of all major records.

http://www.usatf.org/
The official US Track and Field website is packed with information on competitions and athletes.

http://www.spikesmag.com/
A terrific website about athletics with lots of features on the different events and videos of top performers.

http://news.bbc.co.uk/sport1/hi/athletics/skills/default.stm
Watch short videos and animations of how to perform field athletics events at this BBC website.

http://trackfieldevents.com/
This website contains history and details of the technique involved in each field athletics event.

Books
Athletics – Athletics UK, A&C Black, 2006
A good companion guide to both track and field athletics.

Inside Sport: Field Athletics – Clive Gifford, Watts, 2009.
A detailed guide to the different events, the great champions and competitions for field athletics.

Field athletics words

elite top athletes who are usually paid to compete in their chosen sport

Fosbury Flop a technique or way of high jumping in which the athlete heads over the bar head first

landing sector a large, fan-shaped area in which the shot, discus, hammer or javelin must land for the throw to count

O'Brien technique a method of throwing the shot put in which the thrower hops across the circle to build up power

Paralympics an international competition for elite athletes with a disability

personal best an athlete's best ever distance or height for a field athletics event

professional to be paid to compete in athletics

runway the long strip of track-like material which javelin throwers and triple and long jumpers run along before throwing or jumping

scratch line the line on the javelin runway which must not be crossed by an athlete's foot or the throw won't count

stopboard the wooden board at the front of a shot put circle which helps the athlete brake

take-off board a board which runs across the long and triple jump runway. A jumper's foot must be behind the take-off board at the start of a jump

vaulting the action of using a pole to spring from to clear a high bar

Index